Movement Activities for the Early Childhood Classroom

18 lesson plans that engage body, mind, and spirit in playful conceptual learning

Miriam Moran Shankman

Preface by: Pamela Betterton

ISBN: 1-4783-7615-5
ISBN-13: 9781478376156

Table of Contents

Preface

    A Calm Presence   1

Introduction

    What is Nitai looking for?   5

    The Theory behind the Movement   9

    Bringing the Lessons to Life in Your Classroom   13

    The Use of Music in the Movement Lesson   15

The Lesson Plans   **17**

    Slow and Fast   19
    Lost and Found in Space   21
    The Foot Book   25
    From Head to Toe   27
    Movement with Balls   29
    Movement with a Bean Bag   33
    Guess How Much I Love You   35
    Alone On the Mat   37
    The Very Hungry Caterpillar   39
    Harold and the Purple Crayon   43
    Exploring   47
    Movement Bites   49
    Feeding the Body with Sunshine (or Moonlight)   53

Essays   55

    Conflict   57

Good Teachers   59
Who Are You and What Are You Looking For?   61
Willing to Change   63

Preface: A Calm Presence

Our nursery school needed a Movement Teacher. We had no idea when we hired Miriam that she would introduce a program that was completely new to us—one that would so satisfactorily fill our need and also teach us new lessons about working with young children. Each lesson plan presented in this book reflects hours of thought and planning and years of experience to inform and enhance them.

Miriam used insights from her mother, our teachers, and her own observations to refine each lesson plan and make the Movement Classes a pleasure for the children and their teachers. We wanted some yoga centered practices to help teach our three and four year olds to control their emotions and actions. One of my favorite memories is of Miriam and the children and lying on their backs, feeling their tummies rise and fall as they listened to their breathing. Everyone loved that part of the class, and it provided understandable strategies that the children could use in all parts of their lives.

Miriam always projected a sense of calm presence, a loving and accepting focus on the children, and set high standards and expectations for them. They recognized her loving and exacting attention and responded to it with both effort and joy. She has the gift of focus when teaching and is intent on how the children are responding. She uses simple, straightforward instructions and suggestions, and gives the children ample time to work out how to put those teachings into practice.

Kay Houston, a long-time University League Nursery School (ULNS) teacher, put it best when she said that at the end of each class, when it was time to leave, Miriam always left the children in a better place than they were at the beginning of the day. It was high praise and well-deserved. The lesson I've learned from Miriam is that content is important, simplicity is vital, but comportment, focus, and calm need to be consciously developed to achieve fine results from each lesson plan.

It makes me wish I could go back to the beginning and revise my teaching methods with this book, using it as the instrument of how to use focus, attention, calm, and seriousness as a tool for teaching. The philosophy in this book is good for a lifetime. Parents and teachers with children of all ages can benefit from Miriam's presentation of a mindful approach to the techniques of working successfully and responsibly with children.

We teachers and parents are the people whose responsibility it is to provide strategies for children to learn in order to cope with their roles in life.

Pamela Betterton, retired ULNS Director
Princeton, New Jersey

To my mother: some of the lessons I learned from her

I dedicate this book to my mother. In a way it is her book, her work, her "recipes" even though the only time my mother put a lesson plan on paper was when she mailed it to me. We did our work over the phone; she explained every-thing in detail, down to the tone of voice I should use, as I wrote down the plans. When I taught my first lessons in 1989, I kept those papers on the woodblocks and kept going back to them for reference. I dedicate this book to my mother, to the love that lived between us, and to all she showed me, taught me, and gave me.

Being that my mother was *my mother*, the professional and personal lessons she offered frequently intertwined. Very little was not personal to my mother. I think it is the same for me. One of the lessons I learned from her was to share who I am with the students. This is the essence of my teaching.

"Give them time," my mother said after every lesson she observed me teaching. "Give them time to experience each activity. Do not rush to the next part. Help them when they need help and stay out of the way when they do not. Give them time to try, to be confused, to be foolish, to fall, and to get up again. It is all a part of learning." As both her student and her child I can attest that she practiced this in both the classroom and in life.

I have learned that teaching is not just giving instructions. Teaching is also having the time, patience, and strength to bear witness to the students' trials and tribulations and accepting the process in which the student molds the material into his/her own, and to contemplate the idea that the state of not knowing *is* the learning laboratory.

My mother taught me that most children—as well as most adults—could truly learn only one concept at a time. She would say, "Decorate it with more stuff to make it fun but remember not to lose sight of the *one thing* you want them to walk away with. Noticing what people do well and telling them what you like about them opens people's ears so they can hear you better," she would say. "It nourishes their souls so they can grow to be more beautiful." My beautiful mother, with her tender heart that lived through the school of hard knocks believed, and told me over and over again, "There are no bad students, only tired and over worked teachers."

Through this book, I hope to pass along to you not only some of my mother's ideas, creativity, and wisdom, but some of her electrifying personality and beautiful spirit.

What Is Nitai Looking For?

I hear Nitai before I ever see him. It is Saturday morning. I am staying at my sister's apartment on the Kibbutz, where I grew up and where most of my family still lives.

Nine o'clock on a Saturday morning during my vacation is definitely too early to be waking up; too early for me but not for Nitai. I wake up to the soft sound of never ending questions and answers coming through my open window from the neighbor's porch. It sounds as though Nitai's parents want him to eat his breakfast, while Nitai just wants to know every possible and impossible thing about his breakfast. When breakfast is finally over, it seems, from what I hear, that the discussion about riding his tricycle takes quite a bit longer than the riding itself.

By the time I am up and out the door the neighbors' porch is empty. I wonder what this boy looks like and who his parents are.

The next day, as I'm coming back from the pool, I see a childhood friend on the neighbor's porch. Asaf was born one day before me and we grew up together and sat in the same class for the first thirteen years of our lives. Next to Asaf on the porch is his son with blond hair, big wide-open eyes, speaking in the same soft voice as yesterday morning. He asks, "Dad, who is she?" and before receiving an answer from dad, he continues to ask, "What is she doing here?" Why is she wearing a bathing suit?" Who is that with her? Does she have a dog?"

I try to ask Nitai a question to make a connection or to be friendly or maybe to show that I understand the game and know how to ask questions too— my mistake for not knowing that Nitai is doing the questioning here. He's not doing the answering right now, and I can't help wondering: is he doing any listening at the moment?

My next encounter with this question master is at a formal observation I am conducting in his classroom. Nitai is four months short of three years old. In a few weeks he will be moving from the Kibbutz toddler classroom to the pre-school class. For now he is one of the older students in his class.

I'm observing forty-five minutes of free-play and story-time in preparation for the subsequent observation of a movement lesson my mother will be teaching in several days.

It is 11:00 a.m. and the children are done playing outside. They are given a quick shower and are sent into the playroom all clean with their wet hair neatly combed. They are to play for the forty-five minutes until lunchtime. Nitai definitely knows I am here. I can see him checking me every so often with a quick look, though he only does this when other children have come over to talk, ask, show me something, or simply to play with me. Nitai is busy playing with one or two children about his age. They do a lot of large motor activities: going in and out of things, running from one side of the room to the other, swinging their bodies, hammering on the toys. Nitai is talking through all of these activities. It seems that he always wonders about something. There's always something that is not clear or that he needs to find out.

Just before lunch, one of the teachers invites children who are interested in listening to a story into the next room. Nitai is definitely interested.

The children are seated in a circle on the floor. Nitai knows the story and seems very eager to help the teacher complete some of the lines. There are also lots of questions to be asked: Why did the lion hide behind the tree? Where is the rabbit's Mother? Why is he white? Where are his clothes?

I wonder what Nitai is looking for. Though he appears highly involved, he is having a hard time sitting still during storytime. However, every time the teacher asks if he would prefer to play in the other room he sits right back down and chooses to stay and listen.

A few days pass and I return to observe the movement lesson. As a senior in the toddler classroom, Nitai seems very familiar with the lesson format. The movement class starts with the same opening every week and Nitai participates in the ceremony with lots of enthusiasm and large movements. Now, the lesson enters a second phase in which new learning takes place. Today, with toilet paper rolls, the children are working on small motor skills. I notice that Nitai is asking for help before he tries. Clutching his rolls tightly in his hands, with no apparent intention to try the assigned activity, he turns to his teacher (my mom) and announces in a loud and demanding voice: "Ruthi, I can't do it."

Toward the end of the lesson, the children are moving more freely about the room. First, they put all the rolls in a big bag; then they move the bag around the room; then the teacher throws the rolls up in the air and the children try to catch them. Nitai gets excited like the other children but, unlike the others, he runs a bit too fast, accidentally knocking into his classmates, which causes confusion and, ultimately, with him ending up on the teacher's lap. She kisses him lovingly and he seems to calm down.

So what is Nitai doing? Is he looking for something that I cannot see or do not understand? Is he looking for something at all? And why did I get so involved?

The Kibbutz educational system is reluctant to label children and postpones doing so for as long as possible. As a result of this policy, Nitai has not been sent to evaluation and, therefore, has not been labeled.

As for myself, I saw Nitai moving fast, using mostly (almost exclusively) large motor movements. I observed his lack of interest in sitting still. I heard him ask many questions. At first I assumed that my fascination with Nitai was a natural curiosity to find out what those wide-open eyes were looking for. I am now less sure it was the mystery that captivated me.

As a movement teacher I see many children. A weekly lesson does not give me as much time to concentrate on each child as I might like. Here, for a few days on my vacation, I had the opportunity to just observe.

When I began to watch Nitai, I believed I would have to discover what he was looking for in order to help him. I believed I would have to find out what it was and show it to him or bring him there. But Nitai showed me that he believes in the questions, in running around and looking.

Nitai reminded me of two things that I easily forget especially when I get busy. The first is to stop and look, to stop and listen; the second is to remember that questions are always as important as their answers.

The Theory behind the Movement

"*Children love movement. For them movement is basic, like food, sleep, and love. Movement is required for physical, emotional, social, and cognitive development.*" *—Ya'akov Gal-Or, Ella Shoval, Rot Lentzer 1983*

Children need to move in order to develop. A large part of early childhood education should be centered in creating opportunities for them to move, explore, and create through movements. Many early childhood environments currently lack these opportunities.

Creating an environment that supports and encourages movement is the core of movement education. In early childhood education, the environment makes up a large portion of the curriculum. An important component of Movement Education is an open space large enough for children to move about using their whole bodies and spirits, and an attitude that encourages freedom and child-directed movement. Children are too often asked to "stop running" and to "be quiet."

A second component for a well-rounded Movement Education curriculum is a creative program combining movement with literature, conceptual learning, music, props, nature, and cultural events and traditions. It is here that we attempt to let the child interact with the whole world as we explore a wide range of subjects like math, fairy tales, astronomy, geography, time, history, relationships, and holidays. We do so with our body, mind, emotions, and spirit, creating a true multi- disciplinary and "wholistic" (from the word whole) learning experience. Well-rounded experiences engage the child on many levels and create a conceptual understanding of life through movement experimentation. In this book I offer simple activities that will open a door to learning experiences full of wonder, exploration, and joy.

The movement education theories I learned from my mother are based on Jean Piaget's studies of young children, and Rudolf Laban's studies of movement. In combining the two schools of thought, this program engages the child's physical, emotional, social, and cognitive self with movement (i.e., body, space, time, and energy elements). The teacher initiates the activity and then works to achieve a balanced interaction and exchange of child- and teacher-directed flow through the work while keeping it as open-ended as possible.

I've come to the frightening conclusion that I am the decisive element in the classroom. It's my daily mood that makes the weather. As a teacher, I possess a tremendous power to make a child's life miserable or joyous. I can be a tool of torture or an instrument of inspiration. I can humiliate or humor, or hurt or heal. In all situations, it is my response that decides whether a crisis will be escalated or de-escalated and a child humanized or de-humanized. – Haim Ginott

The Kibbutz movement in which I lived and learned had an educational system highly influenced by Jean Piaget's work as well as the work of Haim Ginott, an Israeli child psychologist that lived, studied, and worked in the US. The school I attended on the Kibbutz had no tests and operated in a manner that today, in the US, is referred to as the "project approach," which is child-centered, multidisciplinary method that "engages the whole child."

The adults treated us, the children, with respect and kindness and were very much invested in our education. They also expected a lot of themselves and were very invested in their own lives. Learning from their behavior, we did the same. We all addressed each other by our first names. Learning was very much inspired by Piaget's teachings. We conducted our own investigation on the life of bees and ants; we produced our own plays and musicals; we created our own decorations and made messy looking snacks for parties and worked alongside the teachers who guided and assisted us. When more help was needed, the parents were called to join in on the fun. The parents as well as other members in the community often participated in classroom activities to share their knowledge and experiences. Looking back on my own school experience and relating it to my work in early childhood classrooms today, the word "community" comes to mind over and over again. "It takes a village to raise a child" has become a staple mantra today. Are you working to create a community in the classroom? Do you care about what you do and say? Are you invested in your life?

Creating a community relies on a deep understanding of an underlying equality of all members, and the ongoing development and practice of virtue by each individual.

"Great accomplishments seem imperfect" – Lao Tsu

The third influence in my work comes from the theory, philosophy, and my daily practice and study of Tai Chi Chuan, Chi Kung and meditation. The Dao speaks of nature and sees us as part of nature. I have met many early childhood educators that passionately believe in the importance of a strong nature component in their classroom curriculum. As we tune ourselves into nature, we tune into ourselves, and the children. Nature teaches us about an aspect of the world to which many of us have lost a connection. Knowingly or unknowingly we suffer from that disconnect.

My friend and member of the Wampanoag tribe, Stephanie Duckworth, writes in her book *Poneasequa, the Goddess of the Water* about her grandfather encouraging her to get out of the house: "…I forgot, you would rather learn about life from things that are dead and lifeless then from living breathing things that can show you your own path and give you wisdom." I encourage you to go outdoors with the children as often as you can. Find places as natural as you can find; find places with the least human manipulation. Spend time there in free play in addition to teacher- and child-directed exploration.

In the Tai Chi community there is a debate about the practice of Tai Chi by children, while in the early childhood community there is a high level of interest in bringing such practices as Tai Chi, Yoga, and meditation into the classroom. As with most trends, we tend to forget the basics. In this case, is what we are bringing to the children age appropriate? In this book I present lesson plans following both Tai Chi and early childhood age appropriate principles.

Bringing the Lessons to Life in Your Classroom

When selecting the lessons for this book I wanted to ensure that the lessons are easy to read and understand, and can activate a classroom. It is my hope that you can use this book in your own unique way. You are welcome to work any or each lesson plan step-by-step as presented or to change, adjust, and make it your own! Get creative, have fun, and get the children moving!

If a full lesson plan is over whelming to present, choose one activity, the one with which you feel most comfortable, and try it during circle time. See how it works in your classroom. Watch the children's reactions, observe their ideas, and check to see how you feel about the lesson and proceed from there.

Here are a few tips that I found helpful in creating a good movement experience:

- **How you set up the room is half of your curriculum.** Movement lessons need a space large enough to move in, yet small enough not to get lost in. If you are working in your classroom, try to move things out of the way as much as you can.
- **Prepare.** Think through the plan. Adjust it according to your environment and the children you teach.
- **Make sure you have the necessary materials.** Check that the materials work, and that you have enough for all the children. If a book is involved and it is a book with which you are not familiar, read it to yourself before you read it in class.
- **Keep an open mind and watch the children.** How are the children responding to your instructions? What is the level of engagement during the activity? Are the children having a good time? Are the children coming up with ideas of their own? This observation will help you learn and develop the lesson plans. As

you observe, give the children more time to experience the activities.

- **Allow for some messiness and noise.** Life is messy and so is learning. Uncertainty and confusion forces us into the learning process. Add to that some fun and excitement and life feels good. Life is a process and so is learning. Let go of the product. Live in the process.
- **Bring yourself to the lesson and to the moment.** If you find the importance, beauty, and fun in the activity then, more likely than not, the children will too.

The Use of Music in the Movement Lesson

Music—what a wonderful thing. When I was a child, my grandfather would carefully select music for us to listen to together. He quietly guided my listening and told me the stories behind the music as we listened. At my parent's home, music played almost all the time. We listened to classical, movie soundtracks, jazz, and—my favorite—African American female vocalists.

Making music part of the daily curriculum in the early childhood classroom will benefit the children's body, mind, emotions and spirit, and have lasting effects on their personalities and quality of life. Here are some simple ways to incorporate music into your lesson plan:

- **Play music during part of free playtime.** Try to select different kinds of music on different days. Keep your ears open to new styles of music. Create a diverse music collection.
- **Free dance:** Find music that just "asks for dancing" and spend a few minutes every now and then in a fun moving and grooving dance class.
- **Play-a-long:** Find music you like, give everyone an instrument, and play along with the music. You could sing and play or even sing, play, and dance! See if the children can pick music that they would like to play along with as well.
- **Bring a musician to class:** Maybe one of the parents or teachers in the school plays an instrument—ask if one of them would like to play for the children.
- **Bring music into story-time:** *Zin, Zin, Zin, A Violin* by Lloyd Moss and Marjorie Priceman is a great book to enjoy while learning about music and instruments. *Peter and the Wolf* by Sergei Prokofiev

is another great introduction to the world of classical music. Read the book to the children first, then have the children listen to the recording while following along with pictures in the book. These are just two out of many age appropriate books that explore the world of music.

- **About Using Music in the Movement Lesson Plans** Do we or do we not add music? If we choose to use music, how do we select the music? If the idea of finding the right music— or any music—overwhelms you, leave it alone. Music is not necessary for the lesson plans in this book. Most early childhood educators often hear the word movement after the word music and say, "It's a music and movement program." And while music and movement are closely related, they are not the same thing. In the school I attended, in early childhood classes, movement had priority. All the lesson plans in this book can be used without music. It is also good to remember that sometimes we can hear our body and each other better without music playing.

That being said, if you would like to put music into these lesson plans then please do. Make sure to check that your selection will work well with the activity you are about to do. For example, if you want to incorporate music for the "Slow and Fast" lesson, find slow and fast music. More importantly, check to make sure that the music "works." To prepare, you will need to physically move to the music by yourself before bringing it to class.

THE LESSON PLANS

Slow and Fast

Young children will love to move fast. Moving fast is both natural to them and good for them. This lesson will provide the children with an opportunity to enjoy and benefit from fast movements, as well as explore and experience slow movements. The contrast between the two can help to create excitement and fun. You can use the whole plan as one 30 to 40 minute activity or you can pick one or two activities and present them separately.

You will need: A drum for the teacher, rhythm sticks and egg shakers for children.

Optional: Large written quarter and eighth notes (in case you want to add rhythm notations).

Activities

Moving slowly with the whole body:

Play the drum in a steady beat. Let the children enjoy walking to the drum's beat. Encourage the movement of arms, raising knees up high, and putting on a little smile. After a while say the following as you play: "Walk, walk, walk, walk…." Have your voice match the beat. The children may want to say it along with you, creating a wonderful combination of movement, breath, and sound.

Making a musical connection:

Tell the kids, "This will be our slow walking beat today. We will call it 'Ta." Play the music again as the children walk and repeat "Ta" to every drum beat and step. Encourage loud voices and big movements.

Add fast:

Now play a beat twice as fast. First let the children follow the beat with their feet. Next, as you play say, "Run-ning, run-ning, run-ning, run-ning." Tell the children this will be our running note and we will call it "Titi." Ask everyone to repeat "TiTis" as they follow the beat of the drum.

Upper body movement and more repetition:

While seated in a circle, clap hands slowly as you say, "Walking" or "Ta" with the clapping beat followed by fast clapping with "Running" or "Titi."

With an instrument and...more repetition:

Remain sitting in the circle. Distribute rhythm sticks. Play and say "Ta" in a slow walking beat. Invite the children to walk, talk (only saying "Ta"), and play with the sticks all at the same time!!

Repeat the above exercise using egg shakers for "Ti-Ti."

For older children:

Divide the children into two groups: the "Ta" and the "Ti-Ti" (hand out rhythm sticks to the "Tas" and egg shakers to the "Ti-Tis"). Let each group begin to play on their own. Then have them to play together.

A few helpful tips:

Play and say "Ta" or "Ti-Ti". Let the "Ta" start and the "Ti-Tis" come in after 4 to 8 beats. Have an adult work with each group.

For everyone:

No matter what level you reach playing with the instruments, "take the show on the road" by getting up and encouraging children to move their whole bodies along with the instruments. I like to take turns by letting the "Tas" start walking and talking their "Tas" while the "Ti-Tis" remain "frozen." Then the "Tas" freeze and the "Ti-Tis" go on their "Ti-Ti" run. If you wish to try and have the two groups moving simultaneously, I recommend creating a "Ta Train" and a "Ti-Ti Train." Put a teacher at the "engine" to lead the train. Give each train a run on its own first and then try to have them run together as each group plays and says their own beat.

Lost and Found in Space: Finding "A Good Place" with a Chair

If doing all activities in one day is overwhelming, start with just the first one and see how it goes. Remember we are trying to achieve playing in a crowded environment without physical contact between the children.

You will need: A chair for each child, recorded music or a drum or tambourine that you will play for the children.

Activities

Finding *"A Good Place"*:

- Create a space as large as possible and have all the children sit in a corner looking at the open space.
- Start with Level I. The objective is to make sure that each child has as much space around her/himself as the room allows. Continue onto the next level when you feel the students are ready.

Level I:

Place chairs in the open space and invite student to sit, calling one child at a time. You can say: "Here, I have a chair. I will put it here to stand all by *itself*, and not too close to the wall, not to close to another person or the closet. All by *itself* in *A Good Place*. Ashley, come and sit in this chair all by yourself, in *A Good Place*."

Level II:

One student at a time places a chair and sits on it. Teacher: "Here, Joseph, pick a chair and find *A Good Place* for it, where it is all by itself. Not too close to the wall. Not too close to other chairs. All by *yourself* sit on the chair in *A Good Place*."

Level III:

All students place chairs in the open space and sit on them. In most cases, this will be done after you have gone through either Levels I and II or just Level II (if children are on the older side, Level I can be skipped). You say, "Let's see if everyone can take a chair and find *A Good Place* for it. When you have found your *Good Place*, please sit on your chair."

Level IV:

Students find *A Good Place* without a chair. Once you have done this lesson plan in class a few times, you can use this level anytime you want to have the children all spread out in the open space of the room. You say, "Everyone, please find *A Good Place* where you can stand all by yourself, and not too close to any walls, furniture or other children."

Becoming aware of self in space:

- Children are seated on the chairs looking for neighbors close or far. Can they touch my neighbors? Ask the children to name who is close to them, who is far, and bring to their awareness that they have their own space, *A Good Place*, and are not too close to the children seated next to them.
- Invite the children to walk back to the corner where they sat before finding their *Good Place*. Ask them to make sure not to touch any chairs as they walk. While you stand in the corner, ask the children to look at the chairs positioned in the space. Ask the children for their opinions: are all the chairs in *Good Places*? Rearrange chairs if necessary. Before each child returns to his/her chair, have each child point a finger to his/her chair. Instruct them to then follow their finger slowly back.

Moving into the neighborhood:

First: Movement around the chair.

You play the drum (or any other instrument) or recorded music while each child moves around his/her chair. Start with walking forward, walking backward, tiptoeing, running, and jumping. Ask the children if they have other ideas for moving around the chair. When the music/beat stops, the children sit back on their chairs.

Make sure the chairs are still in *Good Places*. If chairs moved during the activity, return them to *A Good Place*.

Second: Movement all around the room.

Same as before, only this time the children move around the whole space while making sure not to touch the chairs or each other. When the music/beat stops, each child returns to sit on his/her chair.

Third: Go to a new chair.

The instructions remain the same as before only this time, when the music/beat stops, each child will sit on the closest chair to him/her. This introduces the whole **new and important concept of sharing**. Children no longer "own" a chair; everyone is sharing space and property now!

I find this exercise confusing for some children. If you find this happens in your classroom, I recommend that you be gentle and kind as you explain the following: "We are now all sharing the chairs and the space. When the music stops, you stop. Look which chair is the closest to you and sit on it. It is ok to sit and share a chair with someone else." If most of the children get it, let the other ones learn from their peers. If most children have a hard time with this third part, let it go for now and try it later in the year. Save the exercise and try this third part of the lesson for later use.

The Foot Book:
Working with the Body

This lesson plan is suitable for all age groups—including adults! It has the potential of feeling like a party, and it can be part of any curriculum relating to the human feet or Dr. Seuss. Though this lesson plan will work fine with shoes on, I highly recommend bare feet.

You will need: *The Foot Book* by Dr. Seuss, music selections, and/or a hand drum or tambourine.

Activities

Read the story:

In a story-time setting, read the story beginning to end. When you are done reading the story, invite the children to stand up and play along as you all follow the story again.

Play the story:

"Left foot, left foot, left foot, Right." Open to the first page. Holding the open book in your hand, read as you tap with your feet and say, "Left foot, left foot, left foot, right." Make your movements large and exciting by using your whole leg. Repeat the line and the movement a few times. Let everyone move around the room in a "left foot, left foot, left foot, right" march. Moving the body in a joyful way is our objective. **Do not correct left and right during the activity.**

"Feet in the Morning." Ask the children to show you what their feet do in the morning. Give each activity a nice long time for play and practice. Some groups

will take this as an opportunity to run as fast and wildly as they can. Other groups may come up with creative ideas (e.g., brushing your teeth. Then ask, "What do your feet do while you are brushing your teeth?").

The same goes for *"feet at night."* Ask, "what do your feet do while you sleep? Can you show me?" Follow with a *"left foot, left foot, left foot, right"* march. Make the marches loud, large, and fun. They are the chorus in this show.

"Wet foot" is a great opportunity for everyone to jump in imaginary puddles. Play the drum or any other instrument to encourage the children to joyfully activate the whole body as they are remembering and enjoying a fun activity from which they are usually asked to refrain.

Follow with "dry foot." Everyone gets an imaginary towel to dry his or her feet.

During *"high foot" and "low foot,"* I challenge the children to create a statue with one foot low to the ground and the other foot high in the air. Switch the feet. Watch for creative ideas in your group.

"Front feet" and *"back feet"* is a nice opportunity to walk on all fours. You can ask the children which animal they would like to be. Give them plenty of time for practice and play.

Every page on this book is an opportunity to be creative, rejoice in the body, and enjoy its abilities. Have a ball!!

From Head to Toe: Age Appropriate Tai Chi for Young Children

This book was recommended to me by one of the teachers at the Nursery School. Turning it into a movement story is as simple as the book itself. The key to the lesson is to give the children time with each page, animal, position, and movement. If you do so it can become a true Tai Chi experience.

You will need: *From Head to Toe* by Eric Carle. That is it!

Activities

Read it:

Read the statement and question on each page like you mean it: "CAN YOU DO IT?"

Do it:

You can choose to demonstrate the movement to the children or let them try on their own. Either option gives the children plenty of time to try the movement. After a few minutes you can enhance and deepen the experience by asking the children to add the sound of the animal to their movements. Ask them to pretend they really are the animal or the baby animal.

Create it:

Be creative. Try each movement yourself. Ask yourself, "How can each of the animal movements enhance and help the children's movements?" For example, the monkey's movement can help to develop coordination between the different part of the body, and the elephant movements are helpful for lower body strength. Explore the animal, its movement and sound on your own and with the children.

Add to it:

- You or the children may want to add some animals/movements that are not in the book.
- You may want to draw your own pictures of animals moving and/or of the children moving as animals.
- You may want to make up a story about the animals, or even turn the story into a play!

Notes:

For the donkey movement, make sure the children are well spaced out in the room so they do not kick each other. If at all possible, do not skip this movement, as it is a good one for the body to practice. The camel movement is wonderful as well.

Movement with Balls:
The Whole World in My Hands

The children are always excited when they see me coming with a big plastic bag full of colorful balls. I use light-weight, medium-sized balls made of soft rubber. I have found them in dollar stores as well as in catalogs. Aside from being so much fun, the balls are great for working on hand-eye coordination, and whole body movement and coordination. At times, when working with the balls, the classroom may look messy, and all about fun and games. I encourage you to look at each child's body and see the important work that takes place. Give them time and let them play—after all that is their work.

You will need: A ball for each child, music selections.

Activities

Free play:

Give each child a ball. Tell them they can move with the ball any way they would like. Select fun and energetic music. A good way to test this is if you feel like getting up and dancing to the music.

Give the children plenty of time to enjoy the balls, and encourage them with words, demonstrating your own movements, and pointing to children who have interesting ideas of movement.

Watch carefully. You can repeat this activity many times during the year. Observe the children's physical, emotional, social, and cognitive development during this simple free-play session. Your observations can then lead you to ideas of activities you want to create and provide to assist and enhance development. Please keep in mind that repetition is very important. Children need to have time to enjoy their accomplishments before being hurried to the next task.

Move and freeze:

In this second stage we are doing the same movements as the first stage, but with one small addition. When the music stops we freeze our bodies. After a few turns you can challenge the children to freeze their bodies as soon as the music stops. In the move-and-freeze game, we are practicing paying close attention by listening, and teaching body and mind to quickly respond.

Throw and catch:

Now it's time for the important practice and development of hand/eye coordination. Show the children how you throw and catch a ball. Let them try throwing and catching. If many of the children are not able to catch, you may give the following hints:

1) Keep your eyes on the ball—all the time! If your eyes know where the ball is, they will tell it to your brain, and your brain will tell it to your hands!

2) Do not throw the ball too high or too far away from the body.

Demonstrate and encourage the children. Practice is important; make it fun! You can sing: "throw and catch, throw and catch, throw and catch the ball" to any simple melody you make up yourself or use the melody from a popular song. Alternately, put on some fun music.

Bounce and catch:

Here we do the same as with the throwing exercise. This time use a downward motion, bouncing the ball on the floor and catching it on the return. Follow the above instructions.

Working with a partner: throw, bounce, and roll

Children three and a half years or older will usually be able to attempt throwing and catching, as well as bouncing and catching with a partner. If that is too difficult, try having the children roll and catch with the partners sitting facing each other (if legs are open in a V shape it will be hard for the ball to roll away.) The older children can practice rolling and catching as well, sitting across from each other with more distance between them.

Give each activity time, remembering that practice is play, and play is practice.

32

Movement with a Beanbag: Balance, Control, and Coordination

This lesson has been very successful in my very young groups. I have taught it to 18-month-old kids. It can also be a very beneficial and exciting lesson for the four and five year olds.

You will need: A beanbag for each child.

Seated Activities

Tapping:

With the beanbag on the floor in front of you, demonstrate a rhythmic beat by tapping your hand on the bean bag. As you tap, say "Tap, tap, tap tap, tap on the bean bag." Repeat it over and over, keeping a steady and exciting beat.

Next, ask the children if they can tap on the beanbag with their foot. Do the same action with a foot, an elbow, and/or a knee. You can show how even a stomach can tap, tap, tap, tap, and tap on the bean bag! Finish the exercise by standing tall and tapping on the beanbag with your foot.

Body tap:

Holding the beanbag in your hand, tap on each body part as you name it: "head, head, head, head." This exercise is very rhythmic but slower than the first one. Find and tap as many body parts as you wish. It is a good way to check which body parts the children are familiar with and/or can name.

Directions:

Put the beanbag on your head. Tell the children that your beanbag knows how to listen. Say, "beanbag, beanbag, please fall right in front of me!" With a tilt of the head forward, let the bag fall in front of you. Ask the children to check if their beanbag can hear, too. Repeat as many times as the children wish. Follow up with: "beanbag, beanbag, please fall behind me." Then, there's my favorite: "Beanbag, beanbag, please fall on my knee!"

Moving around the room activities

"I'm walking with the beanbag on my head"

Everyone puts a beanbag on his or her head. You can put on some mellow music on for this activity although, sometimes I like to speak through it. Gently and slowly to promote careful handling of the bag, I say: "I' — m walking — with — the — bean — bag — on —my — head, - I' — m - walking - with - the - bean - bag - on - my — head." Repeat the phrase as many times as you want in order to provide quality practice. When you sense the moment is right, call out: "BOOM!" as the bean bag falls to the floor. Do the same activity with the beanbag on a foot, shoulder, hand, stomach, back. Have the children recommend another place to put the beanbag.

Balancing:

Create one solid line on the floor with all the beanbags (like a balance beam for the children to walk on). Let the children walk on the beanbag line (barefoot is best for developing both balance and muscle). I usually have each child take a turn while the rest of the group watches (learning takes place while watching others.)

Next, separate the bags in the line, leaving a one foot space between them. Ask the children to walk the line without touching the bags. Although similar to the first line in this activity, the dotted line creates a different challenge for the body and mind.

Guess How Much I Love You: Age Appropriate Qigong for 6 week olds to 8 year olds

Can you think of anything more profound and worth exploring than love? It makes the world go round!! And here love makes a great opportunity for creativity and physical activity.

You will need:

Guess How Much I Love You by Sam McBratney.

Activities

Read the book as you would at story time:

Make it important, personal, and special.

Read and play:

Tell the children you will read the story again and that this time we get to play like the bunnies. After every page, allow enough time for everyone to act out the activity. Lead the children with words and movements; when the rabbit stretches his arms as wide as he can, do so yourself. Give it a few repetitions. Make sure the emotions are present in your voice and actions. Fun will follow! Hop as they hop. Walk all the way down to the river as they do. For a few of the activities you may need to get creative. For example, when the big rabbits swing the baby rabbit you can have the children swing a stuffed animal or just pretend to be swinging a bunny. Talk about ways to get to the moon (they do not have to be realistic ones). End the lesson by pretending to put all the little bunnies to sleep, providing a nice time for some quiet rest.

Comment:

I find that toddlers love to play out this story, as do three and even four year olds. It is also a wonderful activity to do with the parents. Play it with the children alone a few times first so that they can show the parents how it is done.

Alone On the Mat:
Age Appropriate Tai Chi for
Very Young Children

This is my favorite not-so-well-known book for young children. In a very minimalistic way, this book explores space and emotion providing us with the always welcomed opportunity to explore animal movements. I have used this lesson plan with children ages two to five years.

You will need: *Alone on the Mat* by Brian Wildsmith, a large open space, a space rug (I like using a red rug like the one in the book).

Activities

Read:

You may want to read the book for the children beforehand. Whether or not you have previously used the book, make sure to read the whole book before you start playing. Read slowly, drawing attention to each new animal, and to the cat's reaction to them.

Practice:

First, I have the whole group practice being each of the animals. Encourage movements and sounds. Ask the class, "How do baby animals eat? Drink? Move? Allow plenty of time to explore each animal. At times, the kids want to be animals that are not in the story. That is always encouraged.

Play:

Put the mat in the middle of the open space and tell the children, "Now we will tell the story." Ask each child which animal they would like to pretend to be.

After the children decide which animal they would like to be, place them in different corners of the room as far away from the mat as possible (for example, all the cats will sit next to the piano, all the dogs will sit next to the closet, etc).

Start reading/telling the story and invite each animal, in its turn, to come to the mat. Encourage whole body movement and animal sounds as the children move towards the mat.

Draw attention to the "state of the mat" as it gets crowded.

End the lesson with the cats hissing while all the other animals run away.

Note:

It is ok to have more than one of each animal, as well as to pretend to be an animal not included in the book.

The Very Hungry Caterpillar: Conceptual Learning through Literature and Movement

This lesson can be part of many curriculums/projects: nature, seasons, health, nutrition, and animals. As a movement teacher I usually use it in class around Earth Day. It is a perfect example for conceptual learning through literature and movement. Working with our body, mind, emotions, and spirit, we tap into the nature that surrounds us, the nature that is within us, and the connectedness of the two.

You will need: *The Very Hungry Caterpillar* by Eric Carle, a shoelace and a scarf for each child, paper or felt cut into shapes of fruits and vegetables with punctured holes for string (for the caterpillar to go in and out), and music selections.

Activities

Reading the story with a twist:

I first read the story to the children using a caterpillar, made from a simple shoelace (green color is a nice touch, but not necessary). As I tell the story, I move the shoelace caterpillar in and out of all the foods he eats.

Discussion:

With most groups, I follow the reading with a discussion. I try to provoke thought and contemplation from the book material. I ask questions such as, "What did the caterpillar eat? "Why did the food he ate on Saturday make him sick? Why did eating the leaf make him feel better? Where is the caterpillar once the butterfly comes out? Will you turn in to a butterfly when you grow up?"

A Moving Story:

The tiny caterpillar looking for food:

I give each child a shoelace caterpillar, and say, "Let's begin our story. Show me the caterpillar all tiny inside his egg. When you hear the music, come out of the egg and start looking for some food!"

I put on a pleasant, slow musical selection, and encourage the children to move their caterpillar around the room looking for some food. If necessary, I give them suggestions, and/or point to children who have good ideas to contribute. When the time is right, I "sprinkle" the floor with the fruit and vegetable cut outs.

The caterpillars eat:

The children (caterpillars) find the food and sit for a while "eating" as they work on small motor skills while weaving the caterpillar in and out the holes. Give this activity plenty of time. Remind the children of all the foods the caterpillar ate. Encourage them to do the same.

The caterpillars create a cocoon:

When it seems to you that the caterpillars have eaten enough, change the music to exciting, energetic music for spinning. Tell the children it is time to spin their cocoons. Give each child a big scarf as you take away their shoelace. The children will now be spinning their cocoon to the music. Again, allow plenty of time for this activity. This should be a fun and exciting activity that brings release after the concentration required in the last activity.

The caterpillars turn into butterflies as they rest in the cocoon:

When the cocoons are ready again, change the music to a relaxing restful sound. Remind the children that the caterpillar stayed in the cocoon for more than two weeks. Talk them quietly and softly into relaxing their bodies and resting.

The butterflies push out of the cocoon and fly:

When the rest period is over, remind the children to first nibble a little hole in the cocoon and then push their way out of it. Have a loud, lively fun music selection ready for drying the wings and then flying. Again, allow enough time. Have the butterfly stop at times on a flower or to meet a friend. It's springtime!

Harold and the Purple Crayon: More Conceptual Learning through Movement and Literature

This was the first moving story I did in the classrooms at the University League Nursery School in Princeton in the early 1990s. I had the support of two amazing women: My mother, who mentored me and gave me her life's work, and Pam Betterton, the school director who believed in me, planted me in her school, and showed me all the ropes, the corners, and the ways and means in the American early childhood education world. To date, this remains my favorite movement story.

Harold is a problem solver in real time and I think I am, too. I find wonderful life lessons in this book and I love bringing them to the children.

As you will see I have three recipes for Harold; the middle one has physical movement while the first and last have a different kind of movement. Take the time—this is a classic!

Suggestion: Space the lesson plans. Give a week between them or at least a few days.

Lesson plan one:

You will need: *Harold and the Purple Crayon by Crockett Johnson*, a very large piece of white poster board, and a purple crayon for each child.

Activities

Reading the story and talking about it:

Read the story nice and slowly, giving the children time to absorb all the different twists and turns. When I'm done reading I ask the children question about the story. The idea is to provoke thought about Harold like, how old is he? Is Harold a baby? Then I ask questions that pertain to the storyline like, why did he draw the dragon? Why did he draw nine pies? Could you eat nine pies?

Drawing a story:

Give each child a very large piece of paper and a purple crayon and tell them that now (just like Harold) they will draw their own story. Give plenty of time and encouragement.

Telling the story:

When everyone is done drawing, ask who would like to show and tell his or her story. Each child will get a turn to share the story they drew.

Lesson plan two

You will need: The book, a short wooden stick for each child, background music. **Optional**: other props, such as hoola hoops for a boat and/or a hot air balloon.

Activities

Reading the story and talking about it:

Today, read the story again but only to the part where Harold lands the balloon. Stop there. Ask thought-provoking questions. This time, focus more on Harold's ability to solve problem. What did Harold do when he realized he was in trouble? Why did he do that?

Moving the Story:

Today, give each child a short wooden stick (pretend crayon). Tell the children that when the music is playing they will draw their story in the air with their "make believe" crayon. You can let the children move around and create their own stories in the air or on the ground for a while, and then you can pick selections from the story and have the children move and draw them as you are telling the story. Some of the children may want to make up a short story and tell it. Remember that the goal is enjoyment that comes from the combination of storytelling, problem solving, creativity, surprise, excitement, and physical movement. Take your time; there is a lot lot of learning to be done here!

Lesson plan three

You will need: *Harold and the Purple Crayon by Crockett Johnson*, as many woodblocks as you can get, and a wide open space.

Activities

Reading the story and talking about it:

Start reading the story at the same spot you ended reading it in lesson plan two. Start where Harold lands the balloon in the front yard, and read to the end of the story. Follow with a discussion about how Harold found his home. Ask the children if they can find their home. How will they know it is their home and not someone else's?

Building the story:

Tell the children that today they will build their own home. Ask them to think what they would like their home to have. Would they like it to be like their home or different? Would they have their own room or will they share a room? Would they have a yard? A dog? Where would the kitchen be?

When ready, space out the children so each child has a "property" to build on and ask them to pick out the right blocks for their home. You may need to monitor a bit to make sure that everyone has to have plenty of blocks to build with.

A walk around the neighborhood:

When everyone is done building, take the children for a walk around the neighborhood. Each child will get to show and tell about the house he or she built. With some children you may need to ask questions, others will have plenty to say.

Exploring:
Ears and Hearing

You will need: *The Ear Book* by Dr. Seuss, a selection of music with nature and animal sounds, and an assortment of instruments such as a drum, maracas, a triangle, rhythm sticks, a tambourine, a wood block, a bell, etc.

Activities

Read the book:

Start by reading *The Ear Book* by Dr. Seuss. It is a fun way to introduce the subject of hearing. Begin by asking the following questions: What do we hear? Let's be very quiet and listen—what did you hear? Which part of our body does the hearing? Close your eyes and listen. Do you hear better with your eyes closed? (It is ok if the children do not know the answers). Now try covering your ears. What happened?

Where is the sound coming from?:

Ask the children to stay seated, close their eyes (no peeking!) and point with one finger to where the sound is coming from. Take one instrument and move to different spots in the room. At each spot stop and play the instrument. No peeking!!!

Different sounds—nature and animals:

Using your nature and animal sounds music, play a selection for the children. Ask them to stay quiet and listen carefully until the sound ends and then ask if they can tell you what was making this sound. You can also try to imitate each sound with your voices.

Different sounds—instrument:

Now, using your basket full of instruments, play each instrument. Ask the children to pay attention and listen carefully. Ask them to listen to each instrument with their eyes closed. What does this instrument sound like? What do they like/not like about the sound?

Show the children two instrument they have already heard. Tell them to close their eyes and guess which instrument you played.

Orchestra and audience:

Divide the children into two groups (orchestra and audience). Each child in the orchestra group receives an instrument. Ask the orchestra to play and the audience to listen. After a few minutes, pause and ask the audience what they heard. You can ask the following questions: Did you hear all the instruments? Were some instruments louder than others? Did it sound like something you know? Repeat the experience, and this time ask the audience to close their eyes and listen. Ask if they heard better or differently with their eyes closed. Now switch the groups.

Putting the sounds into the body:

Find some fun or exciting music and tell the children to listen carefully and let the music come into their body and move it—it's dancing time!

Resting and listening:

I like to end this session with the children lying down, eyes closed, body and mind resting and listening to a beautiful nature sound, such as a waterfall, or the ocean.

Movement Bites:
Movement, As Simple As Can Be

This is a collection of short but meaningful movement activities that can be used in circle time or as a transition from one activity to the next. If the larger lesson plans are overwhelming, start here with a Movement Bite!

Relax and Reflect:

This activity can be done in as little as 3 minutes or it can take up to 10 minutes. You can use it during circle time, before a meal or snack, or at any other time during the day to calm the students down. The group can sit, lie down or even stand.

Instruct the children to sit, close their eyes, and take three deep and long breaths. Slowly and softly say, "Innnnnnnnn and outtttttttt, innnnnnnn and outtttttttttt, innnnnn and outtttttttttttt. Now quietly listen to your body, listen to your breath." When you think it is time to wrap up the relaxation exercise, say something to conclude the experience. For example: "I am grateful for the body, the breath, and the time I have to play."

Step to the beat:

You can use a hand drum, tambourine, or set the beat by clapping your hands. Play an enthusiastic walking beat and encourage the children to walk to it.

Play a game of walk and freeze. All you need to do is play a beat and then, without warning, stop. Tell the children that when you play the beat, they can move, but when you stop so should they! If you have the time you can adapt the activity:

- Try the above using a faster, running beat.
- Play very quietly while you tip-toe and invite the kids to join in.
- Choose another instrument to signal crawling on the floor.

Pretending:

Find music that you enjoy and think will work well for pretending to be…an airplane, or a monkey, a river, or a great big dinosaur. Play the music. Tell the children, "Let's pretend we are a great big airplane flying way up high in the blue sky." Continue improvising a storyline, like the following: "Now it is cloudy and the airplane begins to fly through a storm." Perhaps you can encourage the children to turn into small airplanes that make buzzing sounds. Use your imagination and keep it open for ideas the children generate. Follow their ideas, and build on them. Make the movements expressive and fun by incorporating sounds, changing the story lines, and using ideas from as many children as possible.

Balloons:

This game of "follow the leader" begins by having you, the teacher, bending your knees and bringing yourself as close to the ground as possible. Slowly "inflate" yourself. Fill yourself up with air and pretend to grow taller and larger, using your arms and legs to exaggerate how large and filled with air you can get. Keep repeating the following: "I am a balloon, filling up with air, growing bigger and bigger and even bigger than that!"

Pretend to "float" in the air, saying, "I am so big and so light, and I float alllll around the great big sky… I float here, I float there, I float everywhere."

To wrap up this activity, pick from the following two options:

- Produce a great big loud "BOOM!!!" Pretend to burst yourself and fall to the floor, exclaiming – "all done!"
- Deflate yourself very slowly as you move around the room creating a wind like sound, getting smaller and smaller. Lie on the floor and pretend to be deflated.

The children join along with you in the fun. In my experience, they always want to act out the balloon deflating over and over again!

Feeding the Body with Earth Energy:

Tell the children that "all of us will be going together on a march to collect the energy from the Earth. We will bring the energy through our feet into our bodies, so that our bodies can become strong and connected to the Earth like the trees!" First you may want to demonstrate and do the activity with the children. Once they become familiar with the movements, you may want to add some spirit and fun to the activity by playing the drum. Play a beat the children can step to. Remind them to focus on the energy coming from the Earth through their feet, feeding their bodies and making them stronger and more connected to our world.

52

Feeding the Body with Sunshine (or Moonlight)

You can try this activity following *Feeding the Body with Earth Energy* or you can independently use this "bite" of a lesson. Sunshine is an excellent short activity to energize and/or uplift the children's spirits. Use Moonlight if you want to calm or quiet your class.

Make sure each child has plenty of room to stand. Demonstrate by lifting both arms slowly up the sides of your body, "collecting the Sunshine/Moonlight from the sky."Then, slowly lower both arms in front of the body as you bring the Sunshine/Moonlight to feed the body. Repeat the movement a few times.

In the school of Tai Chi and Qigong we see ourselves as part of nature. The more we tune ourselves to nature and the more we follow nature, the more balanced, healthier, and happier we are. In the activities presented here we "feed" our body with energy from different element in nature. Each element has different qualities. We can see Earth as grounding, stabilizing, and nursing, the Sun as energizing and stimulating, and the Moon as calming and relaxing.

Essays

Conflict

I recently read that facing conflict is how we learn.

Many times I did all I could to avoid a conflict, only to end up experiencing it in some twisted way.

Can conflict be avoided?

Should conflict be avoided?

Many times I created a conflict. Did I create it in order to learn something? Or, did I create it in order to avoid something?

I also read that we should always meet conflict with compassion. Well, many times I did not.

One tricky thing about conflict is that many times I do not see it coming, or even recognize it when it is there. I may feel like I am "having a hard time" or more likely that someone is "giving me a hard time." Sometimes the conflict is within me and there are no other people involved.

Understanding the process, existence, and energy of conflict within and around me is how I learn. Do the children you work with learn from their conflicts? Do you allow them the time and space to have conflicts and work them out? Do you observe their conflicts and learn from the observation?

58

Good Teachers

Good teachers are hard to find, and true masters are even harder.

I am thankful for the three years I spent driving up to a Tai Chi farm in Warwick, NY every Saturday morning to participate in Master Jou's Tai Chi class.

Master Jou (81 years old in 1998, the year he died) believed that each one of us was our own teacher. His guidelines were always simple and short, directing me, his student, back to the drawing board to figure out how I can make the material work for me.

Born in China in 1917, Master Jou learned, practiced, played, and taught the art of Tai Chi Chuan during the second half of his life.

Over the years I have heard Master Jou repeat over, and over, and over, and over...:

Know yourself

Do your best – Don't overdo

Nothing serious

A little adventure

A little smile

Graceful – like a dancer, fierce – like a martial artist

Make a little progress

Good structure - Full spirit

No secret, just hard work

How will your students remember you? What lessons are you giving them? What is it that you want them to remember most?

Who Are You and What Are You Looking For?

In *The Wizard of Oz*, each one of the four main characters is looking for something. They join each other on a journey in search of The Great and Powerful Oz, who they believe can give them what they think they are missing.

The Scarecrow is looking for a brain.

The Tin man is looking for a heart.

The Lion is looking for courage.

And Dorothy is looking to get back home.

Which one of these characters is most similar to you?

What are you looking for?

Are you like the scarecrow looking for your brain? Or like the Tin man, looking for your heart? Are you like the Lion (and me) looking for courage? Or are you like Dorothy, looking to get back home? Maybe you have a different issue, one that did not show up in the movie, or a combination of two or more.

Are you on a journey to find what you are missing?

Or

Are you on a journey to find a wizard who can give it to you?

And what about the wizard's advice at the end of the movie?

Could it be that you've always had what you're looking for and just didn't know it?

And the children you work with, what are they looking for? Can you find the time—a minute or two—to quietly stand on the side and listen to their words and their wishes? Watch their moves, gestures and energy. Who are they? Who do they wish to be? Who will they become?

Willing To Change

I am willing to change with the times.

Not because of the styles and trends that are constantly changing, but because **I am changing**.

I am willing to change with the times, and it is a great help in my relationships with children.

A friend once told me that, looking back on the years when her children were young, she often felt she was a step behind. They were changing and she was playing catching up.

In *The Bucket List,* Carter says, "45 years pass so fast," to which Edward replies, "Like smoke through a key hole."

Let me be the smoke, majestically flowing throw the key hole, and not left behind.

Set up the game.
Observe all players' moves.
Be willing to change.

CPSIA information can be obtained at www.ICGtesting.com
Printed in the USA
LVOW08s0233070714

393135LV00003B/198/P